Original title:
The Glimmer of Glasses

Copyright © 2025 Creative Arts Management OÜ
All rights reserved.

Author: Adrian Caldwell
ISBN HARDBACK: 978-1-80586-017-4
ISBN PAPERBACK: 978-1-80586-489-9

Through Crystal Lenses

Oh look, my nose has grown quite wide,
Through lenses thick, I try to hide.
A fly on the wall, I shall report,
But wait, is that a dancing tort?

The Light That Bends

With every turn, the world is strange,
A dog walks tightrope, I must arrange.
My cat in a tux, oh what a sight,
Wearing my specs, she thinks she's bright.

Spectacles of Time

I peek through frames, the clock is slow,
A snail wears boots, ready to go!
I'd toast to time with a limp wrist,
But first, I've lost my specs—oh, a twist!

Echoes of Clarity

In the realm where laughter springs,
Each joke a bell that brightly rings.
I see you now, with googly eyes,
A prince or a fool? I can't surmise.

Through the Lens of Memory

Reflecting moments, so absurd,
A cat in socks, I once heard.
The past is funny, twisted in time,
Like a clown on a unicycle, oh so prime.

Forgotten laughter, ringing clear,
What was so serious is now quite deer.
Old dice rolls from nights of fun,
Now just stories that barely run.

A Canvas of Transparency

Pictures painted in shades of cheer,
A mustache drawn on my buddy's rear.
Every sip taken brings a new jest,
Like juggling oranges, we're at our best.

Transparent tales, they just don't fade,
A wardrobe malfunction, quite a charade.
The tales we weave are bright and bold,
Like socks with sandals, a sight to behold.

Rays of Forgotten Thoughts

Ideas flicker like fireflies bright,
I once tried dancing in the moonlight.
A memory tickles my funny bone,
Like a penguin wearing a tweed cone.

Lost in a daydream, swirling with glee,
Recalling the time I climbed a tree.
I slipped and fell, but felt quite grand,
With splinters in places I'll never understand.

Gleaming Perspectives

Looking through laughter, everything's clear,
Like a parrot squawking with no sense of fear.
With giggles and chuckles, we spin and twirl,
Each foolish moment, a joyous whirl.

Reflect on life's quirks and blunders galore,
Like wearing mismatched shoes at the store.
It's the quirky mishaps that paint our fate,
In a gallery filled with humor, it must be great!

A Glance of Hope

In a world where we squint, oh so slight,
A hopeful gaze turns wrong to right.
With lenses thick and frames askew,
We find our joy in absurd view.

We wear them tilted, we dance and sway,
Making woes vanish, come what may.
Through blurry edges, we laugh and cheer,
For joy's a vision, always near.

Visions Through Fractured Glass

Peering through cracks, a jester's delight,
What's lost in focus brings giggles of light.
Each pane a puzzle, a riddle to spin,
We see our mishaps and burst out in grin.

Hats on our heads, but shoes on the wrong,
Our twisting reflections just can't be wrong.
Tripping through frames, we frolic and dance,
In silly distortions, we take our chance.

Shimmering Perspectives

Wearing shades both close and wide,
New angles make me laugh inside.
What's near is distant, what's far is close,
Each glance a treasure, we'll laugh the most.

The world is painted in wobbly hues,
A merry-go-round of silly views.
From crooked noses to grinning mouths,
We find in fun what laughter's about.

Chasing Reflections

Running in circles, can you see?
The funhouse mirrors, oh, let it be!
Images bouncing, we stumble and fall,
In a world of laughter, we conquer all.

With every twist, our smiles expand,
A sprightly dance, hand in hand.
For every echo, a giggle in tow,
Chasing reflections, we steal the show.

The Dance of Transparency

Beneath the sun, they twirl and sway,
A pair of specs in a quirky ballet.
They leap and hop with a gleeful cheer,
Who knew they'd steal the show right here?

Frames that wiggle, lenses that gleam,
They slip and slide like a funny dream.
Each twist and turn, a sight to behold,
In their wacky dance, the world feels bold.

Hues of the Heart's Eye

With rosy tints, they find the fun,
Like clowns on parade in a marriage run.
A kaleidoscope of laughter, oh so bright,
Colors collide in pure delight!

Through these prisms, the world's a joke,
Every stare ignites a playful poke.
With a wink here and a grin right there,
Reality's absurdity fills the air!

Light-Catching Memories

Reflections of past that glint and glow,
Each glance a giggle, each blink a show.
Captured moments with a touch of grace,
In this quirky world, there's no sad face!

A chuckle here and a chuckle there,
As laughter dances in the evening air.
Through shiny frames, the tales spill out,
Of silly mishaps, without a doubt!

Radiance in the Ordinary

In simple styles, the humor thrives,
A dash of wit in our daily lives.
They catch the light with every glance,
Making mundane moments do a dance.

A smudge, a streak, oh what a sight,
These specs play tricks, oh what a delight!
In the ordinary, they find the cheer,
Glasses that laugh as the world draws near.

Brilliance in Quiet Moments

A sparkle caught in morning light,
I sip my tea, what a delight.
The world is vibrant, colors burst,
In cozy silence, I feel the thirst.

My spectacles perched upon my nose,
They see my thoughts, I think, who knows?
Laughter dances with every glance,
In playful moments, I find my chance.

Secrets Behind Shiny Frames

Behind the lenses, secrets lie,
Through curious eyes, I dare to spy.
What tales do they hold, what dreams they share,
In a world that sparkles, beyond compare.

A wink, a nod, a silly grin,
The frames reflect where fun begins.
Donning my specs with flair and charm,
Life's little quirks, they help disarm.

Shattered Reflections

Oops! There goes my clumsy hand,
The floor's a stage for glassy sand.
With pieces scattered, laughter's near,
Who knew the floor could be so sheer?

In every shard, a joke ensues,
Reflections of silliness in hues.
I wear my mask of broken pride,
And chuckle at my wild ride.

Prism of Dreams

In silly shapes, my visions play,
A rainbow twist on mundane gray.
With squinty eyes, the world refracts,
A comical scene, oh, where it acts!

I chase the colors, they dance and weave,
Hoping to catch what I believe.
In laughter's light, I see the fun,
As dreams unfold, my heart's just begun.

Reflective Whispers

In a world where noses do dance,
A pair of lenses takes a chance.
Jokes are clearer, laughter is near,
While squinting friends just disappear.

Mirror reflections show silly sights,
As quirks and quirks bring delight-filled nights.
Who knew a sheen could hold such glee,
Or make the cat look like a bee?

Through Crystal Lenses

A goggle-clad spy with a nose so grand,
Sees the world through a wobbly hand.
With every glance, it's laughs galore,
Like a town crier that fell on the floor.

An old chap trips over an unseen pup,
Only to find he's got his cup.
Through blurry sights, he cracks a grin,
Saying, 'Did I mean to wear these again?'

Spectacles of Distant Dreams

Oh, the far-off sights of a muddled brain,
With visions so wild, they can't feign plain.
Wearing these wonders, I chase mirth,
As noses turn points of comedic worth.

A goggle-eyed friend just spotted a snail,
And proclaimed it a dragon with a mighty tail.
Amidst the giggles, dreams start to swirl,
In laughter's embrace, we gently twirl.

Clarity in Fragments

With cracked glass frames and frayed designs,
Life's amusing puzzles draw funny lines.
Bits of sunlight peek through with flair,
Making old dogs do a curious stare.

Through funny filters, each face a muse,
Nothing's off-limits, no chance to snooze.
A theater of whim, a riotous play,
Where everyday sights lead us astray.

Radiant Impressions

There once was a pair, quite bold and bright,
Their frames made the world feel just right.
They twinkled and sparkled, causing a scene,
With every small glance, they reigned as the queen.

But on Tuesday, oh dear, they took a small dive,
Into a bowl of soup, did they survive?
They emerged with a shine, yet now they reflect,
The flavors of dinner, a curious effect.

The Crystal Nook

In the corner they sat, with a charming appeal,
A collection of lenses, oh what a deal!
One sat on a cat, thinking it could fly,
While another told secrets to the passing pie.

The dog eyed the pair with a puzzled look,
As they told thrilling tales from each little nook.
With giggles and snorts, they polished their sheen,
Creating a ruckus, a scene most obscene.

Cascading Colors

A flicker of fun, in hues all around,
As each lens caught light, they danced on the ground.
Like rainbows on ice, they spun and they turned,
In the laughter of optics, each moment was learned.

A peep through the red, oh what a surprise!
A chicken in boots with bright polka dot ties!
While green made a frog, quite dapper and neat,
Admiring his style with a tap of his feet.

The View Through Time

With a wink and a twist, they traveled through years,
To watch silly moments and shed joyful tears.
They saw a grand dance, where a cat wore a hat,
And a mouse on a skateboard fell down with a splat!

Each glance brought a chuckle, each squint made them grin,
As tales of high jinks danced round in a spin.
So raise up your frames, let the stories unwind,
For laughter awaits, in each lens you may find.

Light's Gentle Capture

A wink from the sun, quite sly,
Catches a smile from the sky.
Shadows dance in a playful chase,
As the world swirls in a bright embrace.

Tiny flecks spark in delight,
Turning the mundane into a sight.
Each glance reveals a silly face,
In reflections of joy, we find our place.

Laughter bounces off the walls,
Every sparkle leads to giggles and calls.
Frames that twist our serious frown,
In this funhouse, we never drown.

So grab those frames, let's explore,
With every look, there's just more in store.
Life's quirks captured in a playful glow,
Let the light catch us, come on, let's go!

Beyond the Frame

A world beyond a bordered view,
Where silliness takes on a hue.
In playful shapes, our faces gleam,
What lies beyond is a wacky dream.

Upside down or inside out,
What's this fuss? We wiggle about!
With a grin sneaking past the edge,
We leap from frames, a laughing pledge.

The cat wears glasses, quite absurd,
While squirrels chip in, not a word.
Every angle hides a surprise,
In this chaos, our laughter flies.

Join the fun, let's take a peek,
In a realm where whimsy doesn't speak.
Life's a ride, and oh, what a game,
Beyond the frame, we're all the same!

In the Depths of Clarity

In the depths where vision plays,
Silly pictures brighten our days.
Every glance, a twist of fate,
Seeing the world in a delightful state.

Fish in shades, wearing hats,
Reading books, oh, how they chat!
Through the lens, we jump and cheer,
Creating scenes that tickle the ear.

Mice in suits, oh what a sight,
Dancing under the golden light.
With every gleam, there's laughter shared,
In our quirky giggle fest, none are scared.

A wink from the silly and bright,
Turns the mundane into pure delight.
In this clarity, all is bright,
Join the fun, laugh with all your might!

Mirrored Realities

In mirrors where mischief collides,
Reflections burst with silly guides.
Each glance reveals a funny foe,
As our quirks put on quite a show.

Chickens strut with glamor and flair,
While cows do yoga without a care.
Through this lens, life takes a twirl,
With giggles spilling, let's give a whirl.

Faces morph and colors swirl,
Such nonsense makes our hearts unfurl.
In each mirrored wink, we find joy,
As laughter reigns, the fun we deploy.

So twist and turn through these frames,
In mirrored worlds, we'll play new games.
With every chuckle, the truth we see,
In these realities, we're wild and free!

The Clarity of Light

In a room full of faces, I search for the bright,
But friends say my glasses are giving me fright.
Each smudge and each smudge, they make me a tease,
Yet laughter erupts as we share in the ease.

I squint at my burger, is that pickle or cheese?
They whisper it's ketchup, someone call for a breeze!
The clarity missing makes moments a jest,
As I stumble through life, but I'm still at my best.

Wandering Through Glass

With a swipe of a hand, I clear the fogged frame,
But oh, what a journey this pair is to tame!
I wander through rooms as if lost in a maze,
Hoping to find where I've set the remote blaze.

Each time that I blink, my view shifts and sways,
The cat on the shelf transforms into a vase.
Friends snicker and snort—oh, the sights that I miss,
They know that I'll stumble, and yet they persist.

Discovery in Reflection

Why is that a window looks back with a grin?
I swear, my own reflection is playing to win!
I pose and I prance, like a true movie star,
Yet my image just laughs—it's a comical scar.

Every glare from the sun, a new game that starts,
With reflections so wacky, they rattle my parts.
I spot every crack, but I'm not really sad,
In a world full of silliness, life isn't so bad.

The Illumined Path

Through lenses so thick, I navigate night,
Each step is a stumble, oh what a sight!
The trees seem like monsters, or maybe just gnomes,
With flickering lights, I forget all my combs.

My friends shout and giggle, 'Watch out for the curb!'
But I'm on an adventure, my legs all a blur.
Through missteps and laughter, I find my own cheer,
As I dance down the path, fueled by good beer!

Light's Play on Fading Vision

In the drawer, old specs hide,
Time they spent, a jolly ride.
With each twist, the world's a blur,
Like a magic show, absurd for sure.

Searching pockets, lost my sight,
Found a donut—a tasty bite.
In laughter's light, I squint and grin,
What's clear today, I can't begin.

Bright colors dance, then fade away,
Like socks that vanish, day by day.
Through foggy fronts, I take a peek,
As laughter melds with every squeak.

What if fate is just a joke?
A pair of specs I'd gladly poke.
When vision dips, I don't despair,
I'll wear my smile like a flare.

A Spectrum of Memories

In a world so bright yet dim,
Nostalgia's song begins to swim.
Colors flash, then drift away,
Like ketchup stains from yesterday.

Snapping photos, smiles askew,
Caught a glimpse, but missed the view.
Life's a rollercoaster, ups and downs,
While I'm searching for my missing crowns.

Sipping tea in shades of gray,
Conversations start to sway.
Friends all laugh, I join the tease,
Straining hard, I just can't see!

In this haze of silly sight,
Memories sparkle, delightfully bright.
A world of whimsy, crisp and clear,
Where eye twinkles bring us cheer.

Glances that Illuminate

At coffee shops, I miss the mark,
With every look, I miss the spark.
Friends may wave, I wave back late,
Caught in a moment, fate might wait.

Through tinted lenses, I observe,
The world is quirky, full of curve.
With each giggle, new sights awaken,
Reality shifts, slightly shaken.

A sneaky puppy steals my shoe,
I chase him down, it's quite the zoo!
My gaze, it wobbles, all a blur,
But laughter's clear; it's quite the lure.

With each glance, we share a jest,
In this haze, I feel the best.
So I'll wear my shades with flair,
Embracing life—no time to spare!

Fractured Reflections

Mirrors crack as I step near,
What's this image? Oh dear, oh dear!
A funny face looks back at me,
Like a clown from a comedy spree.

Filters fail, the truth appears,
In the shards, I see my fears.
But laughter echoes in the glass,
With every chuckle, my worries pass.

A little twist, a silly pose,
Fleeting moments, who really knows?
Reflections dance, they flip and play,
In this jest, I steal the day.

So here's to laughter, loud and clear,
In fractured frames, we've naught to fear.
Embrace the chaos, let it flow,
In every glance, let joy bestow.

Clarity in Chaos

In a world so wild and bright,
I fumble for my specs, alright.
With each twist and turn I see,
A squirrel doing yoga by a tree.

A cat in shades, looking cool,
Dancing like it's nobody's rule.
I trip on socks, fall to the floor,
Laughing at what I saw before.

Blurriness is my best friend,
It seems to make all colors blend.
But through the fog, a glimpse of cheer,
A pizza slice is always near.

With kaleidoscopic mind and eye,
I wobble like a penguin, oh my!
When all is hazy, fun shall reign,
In this glassy chaos, I'm insane.

The Window's Serenade

Through panes of glass, I often peep,
In sunny plots where squirrels leap.
They chatter on, a funny crew,
Making me laugh 'til I turn blue.

A plant in shades, swaying about,
Claims it can dance without a doubt.
It tips and bends, a quirky move,
Its leaves go jiving, making groove!

The neighbor frowns, looks ever so stern,
While I sip tea, watch the world turn.
With humor bold, I wave my hand,
To the mischief in this glassy land.

Every glance holds a story bright,
A spectacle of lost delight.
Behind the windows, joy's parade,
In my giggly bubble, I've got it made.

Light Falling Softly

When morning breaks with shining grace,
I search for shades to save my face.
With beams that dance, they startling splay,
On breakfast eggs, in a comical way.

Juggling spoons, I make a mess,
Butterflies join, my chaos they bless.
The toast pops up, like it's seen a ghost,
While I laugh at this morning boast.

A shadow play of butter and jam,
Every bite sings a sticky glam.
In the kitchen, goofy is king,
With every splash, the dish sings.

Yet when my specs catch every gleam,
Reality turns into a dream.
As goofiness wraps the day in cheer,
In this soft light, I've nothing to fear.

Fragmented Truths

In a mirror world of quirky sights,
My reflection plays in dazzling lights.
A head of veggies makes me grin,
Each carrot's dance, a silly spin.

Glances flicker, truths left behind,
In jumbled shapes I often find,
A pizza slice that's dressed with flair,
Winks at me from the kitchen chair.

With every word I try to say,
It hops away, without delay.
A jigsaw piece of fractured fun,
In this crazy game, no one has won.

But through the folly, laughter grows,
In fragmented truths, the funny flows.
Embrace the chaos, let it dance,
In this whimsical life, take a chance.

Lenses of Lost Time

In a world where vision's blurred,
Each blink a minor pause,
The clock ticks loud, absurd,
Through frames with broken jaws.

I tripped on facts so clear,
Wearing specs from my teens,
Reality's a sneer,
In these timeless machines.

I tried to see the future,
With lenses cracked in play,
But all I found was suture,
And a gum stuck to my tray.

Each visit to the eye doc,
Is like a circus show,
Trying on a tick-tock,
With laughs at every row.

Delicate Hues of Insight

With colors sharp and bright,
I squint through borrowed hue,
Pretending to feel right,
While stepping in a shoe.

I thought I saw a rainbow,
But turned out just a kite,
Betting on my clever throw,
To gain some mental height.

Wearing shades indoors now,
To look both cool and wise,
But friends just laugh and how,
At these peculiar ties.

My visions twist like pretzels,
In frames of tangled thoughts,
The insight's just confetti,
Mixed in with all my blots.

Radiant Veils of Understanding

Silly stories flicker bright,
Beneath my clumsy frames,
Where truth and jest unite,
Like oddball memes with names.

With friends I share this vision,
As laughter fills the air,
In every wild decision,
We wear our craziest flair.

Each pair shows parts of me,
Reflections oh so bold,
A custard under the sea,
In crystals made of gold.

With jokes wrapped tight in glass,
I search for hidden gems,
But clarity's a mass,
Of giggles and extremes.

Windows to the Soul's Palette

In frames of every size,
I spy a painted wall,
Each brushstroke is a prize,
In this whimsical hall.

Look at me and you will see,
The colors of my plight,
From green to polka dots,
In this chaotic light.

A kaleidoscope of dreams,
Flashing past in haste,
With giggles, wiggles, beams,
And a side of whipped paste.

Each glimpse a comic strip,
Of thoughts that swirl and dance,
Oh, the wildest trip,
In these frames I take a chance.

The Lens of Yesterday

Once I found a pair so bright,
They turned my world into a sight.
My cat wore them, slipped and fell,
Now I see what I can't tell.

My friend thought he could read a tome,
With specs that looked like a garden gnome.
He bumped his nose on a doorframe,
And yelled at me, but who's to blame?

A smudge on glass, a mystery's tease,
Makes me wonder, 'Is it me, or fleas?'
With lenses thick, I see too well,
The state of chaos in my shell.

In silly shapes, they make me grin,
With every glance, let the fun begin!
Through twisted frames, I shout with glee,
Life's just a joke; can't you see?

Reflections of a Dream

Woke up with dreams stuck on my face,
A mirror showed me in a weird place.
My specs were cracked, yet I still viewed,
A world where cats in suits just mewed.

At breakfast time, I wore a haze,
Saw eggs and toast in a crazy blaze.
The butter danced, the coffee flew,
In glasses, funny sights ensue.

With every blink, a new surprise,
Like floating donuts or dancing pies.
A world absurd, so wild and bright,
Through funny frames, all takes flight.

As I adjusted, laughter rang,
In wacky visions, life was slang.
Chasing whimsy, lighthearted schemes,
The world unfolds; oh, what a dream!

Illuminated Vistas

Searching for views that make me laugh,
I donned some lenses that did the math.
Trees wore hats, and clouds held pets,
While I stumbled on my morning bets.

Each glance revealed a comical show,
A banana boat on the street below.
I chuckled hard at squirrels in ties,
They traded stocks, to my surprise!

The flowers danced in pirouettes,
As butterflies played see-and-sets.
A cat juggled with a curious grin,
While I watched on, wearing my din.

Through frames of frolic, the day spun round,
In absurdity, delight is found.
Laughter leaped from every view,
With silly sights, the world feels new!

Hallowed Glass

In a corner shop, I found the prize,
A pair of specs with cosmic ties.
They promised to reveal the truth,
Instead, they showed me my lost youth.

I wore them once, and what a scene,
My last haircut looked like a machine.
The mirror laughed as I stared back,
This style was truly off the track.

Reflections glimmered at my side,
A talking lamp became my guide.
With silly banter and clever ease,
We paraded through the farcical breeze.

In this hallowed sight, I learned to play,
With winks and laughter to fuel the day.
Through funny lenses, life's no bore,
With each glance forward, I crave more!

The Hidden Depths

Behind the lens, what do we see?
A world that's funny, wild, and free.
A cat in a hat, a dog in a shoe,
Who knew such wonders could come into view?

Each scratch and smudge, a new fun tale,
With laughter that dances, never to fail.
Unruly reflections, a clown's piercing stare,
The magic is hidden, but we all must beware!

A toast to the quirks that lenses reveal,
Where silliness bursts, a comedic zeal.
Spectacles shining, bright as a star,
Where humor and chaos mix without bar!

So lift up your frames, don't take life too tight,
For through those odd arcs, we find pure delight!
In this wacky world, using each glass,
The punchlines abound, and the moments amass!

Vistas of Light

Through the glass, the sun gleams bright,
Transforming the mundane into pure delight.
A squirrel in boots catches my gaze,
While the trees dance, lost in their plays.

Reflective surfaces twist the mundane,
A chicken in glasses? Oh, what a gain!
With each wink and blink, the visuals shift,
In the comedy show, the world has a gift!

Oh, silly shapes, unkempt and absurd,
Where laughter erupts, without a word.
We navigate life, with quirky delight,
Turning glances into outrageous light!

So grab your spectacles, let's share a laugh,
In this whimsical world, we'll carve our own path.
A glimpse here, a peek there, so much to explore,
With each vista of wit, there's always more!

Portal of Perspectives

Look through the portal, what do you see?
A pig in pajamas, sipping some tea!
The world spins around, in delightful array,
Where silliness reigns, brightening the day.

Curved edges reflect our chaotic views,
Turning drab moments into vibrant hues.
A laugh with a wink, reality's twist,
Funny how life has a comedic gist!

Through swirling glass, a merry-go-round,
Hilarity waits at every sight found.
With laughter as currency, there's value in fun,
What treasures emerge when we're all on the run!

So, peer through the lenses, engage in this game,
Where every odd vision holds a quirky name.
In this portal of play, we can't help but grin,
For the laughter of life keeps drawing us in!

Gazes That Shift

With glasses askew, the world seems so strange,
Laughter erupts as the sights rearrange.
A rabbit in sneakers takes a wild leap,
While a cloud with arms starts counting sheep!

In this viewfinder, each giggle ignites,
From owls in tuxedos to cows with kites.
Shifting perspectives, the absurd takes flight,
Bringing joy that dances, oh what a sight!

Over the frames, just let out a snort,
For laughter is fuel, a hilarious sport.
At every turn, we're met with a grin,
Through lenses of whimsy, let the fun begin!

So join in the joy, embrace the bizarre,
With gazes that shift, we all shine like stars.
In this giggling kaleidoscope, ideas collide,
Where humor and life are forever allied!

The Whisper of Glass

In a cafe, sipping tea,
I catch a glimpse of me.
My friend with specks of foam,
Claims the cup feels like home.

I wave my hands in glee,
Knocking over his green tea.
He laughs, I start to frown,
As the chaos spins around.

His specs now a fishy stew,
From the spill, a vibrant hue.
With a giggle, I take a peek,
At the cleanup, oh so meek!

Through the lenses, we now see,
A wild world, so carefree.
Making memories through the haze,
Of laughter-filled, silly days.

Hues of Hindsight

Looking back with silly pride,
At moments that can't hide.
My glasses, thick as a book,
Help me see the goofy look.

That time I wore them upside down,
Felt like the funniest clown.
I thought they helped me focus,
But turned my world ferocious!

Bright colors of my past emerge,
Each memory starts to surge.
With laughter, I raise a toast,
To the ones I love the most.

Through awkward frames, we find delights,
In all our silly sights.
With hindsight's playful tease,
Life's just a laugh, with ease.

Chasing Fleeting Moments

A butterfly caught my eye,
Zooming fast in the sky.
Swatting with my glasses near,
I toppled over, oh dear!

Moments flutter, quick and bright,
Fleeting gems that feel just right.
I chase them with all my might,
And fall into fits of delight.

In my frenzy, I forget,
That laughter is no regret.
With my lenses full of cheer,
I embrace every silly tear.

Now every mishap makes me grin,
Each stumble a glorious win.
As I chase the time that flies,
With giggles as the grand prize!

The Dance of Reflections

Mirrors dance in playful queues,
Mimicking my silly moves.
A twirl, a spin, I laugh aloud,
With echoes bouncing through the crowd.

Onlookers chuckle at my flair,
As I trip on the air.
My glasses got the floor all wet,
A slip and slide? It's a bet!

Through the glass, we start to see,
A world of jests and harmony.
In every bounce and silly play,
Life's a dance in a funny way!

Join the fun and take a glance,
At the art of silly dance.
For reflections lead to smiles,
Making every moment worthwhile!

Illuminated Whispers

When frames appear so grand,
You'd think they have a plan.
They sit upon my nose,
As if they know who chose.

In every laugh and grin,
They catch what lies within.
Like spies in bright disguise,
Always judging my wise.

They twinkle in the light,
Causing quite the sight.
My friends just roll their eyes,
While I look like I fly.

With each sunbeam I chase,
A new and funny face.
So here's to every lens,
That turns foes into friends.

Reflections in Stillness

In my frames, the world's a mess,
I see every kind of dress.
People prancing around,
While I just stand my ground.

A smudge here, a streak there,
I laugh at what I wear.
Those reflections come alive,
As my humor starts to thrive.

Oh what joy these sights can bring,
Like a circus on a swing.
I may be nearsighted, true,
But I see life in a hue.

So here's a toast with cheer,
To the laughter that draws near.
In the stillness, I will sway,
My glasses have their own play.

Fleeting Light's Promise

I slip these frames with glee,
To see what's right in front of me.
A world that's full of grace,
Looks odd in this bright space.

Around me colors dance,
Every glance a chance.
I chuckle at the sights,
In this chaos of delights.

The light gives way to fun,
Like a game that's just begun.
Each moment, quite absurd,
With reflections that are stirred.

With every witty line,
These frames are simply divine.
I'll wear them with a grin,
For the laughter to begin.

Infinity in Focus

Through these lenses, I explore,
Infinite jokes galore.
Each twist and turn I chase,
In this wacky, wild space.

A blurry tale, a clear joke,
Hilarity in every poke.
I'm the captain of this ship,
On laughter's jubilant trip.

Every friend shares a glance,
And together we'll dance.
With frames perched on our nose,
We navigate through prose.

So raise your glasses high,
To the spirits that can fly.
In this life, in such a mess,
We find joy, we confess.

Fragments of Vision

In a world that's bright and bold,
Silly sights begin to unfold.
With squints and winks, we see it clear,
Oh, how we laugh, oh, how we cheer.

Once I saw a cat in socks,
Dancing 'round like tricky clocks.
Mismatched shoes, a fashion blunder,
Who knew sight could bring such wonder?

Through layers thick, my view is strange,
Every face seems to rearrange.
I thought my friend was a giant chef,
Turns out he's just himself, no improv left.

With each new glance, I shake my head,
My vision's gone, or so it's said.
But in this haze, the jokes emerge,
Life's little quirks, they truly surge.

Windows to Wonders

Peer through the frames, what do I see?
A bird in a tie sipping herbal tea.
Squirrels in suits, oh, such a sight,
Chasing each other, what a delight!

I saw a dog lead a parade,
With hats and banners, they weren't afraid.
Every tail wagged to a silly beat,
In this world, joy is quite the feat!

Gnomes in the garden throw a rave,
Under the stars, they dance and wave.
With every wink from my frame of view,
Reality laughs, oh, how it grew!

Round these windows, the stories flow,
Funny antics beneath moon's glow.
The wonders peek with each glance shifted,
In laughter's arms, our spirits lifted.

A Dance of Light

Oh, watch the rays as they prance and play,
They tickle the ground, making shadows sway.
A squirrel does ballet upon a log,
While lampshades tremble, the dance is a hog!

Light twists and twirls, a jolly show,
With every flicker, it steals the glow.
I swear I saw a bright light mime,
A chatty bulb cracking jokes on a dime!

In the kitchen, forks begin to jig,
As spoons join in, doing a gig.
With every shine, the laughter spreads,
Can't stop smiling at the light that treads!

The chandelier spins with glee and grace,
Reflecting joy, it lights the place.
In this dance of hues, the fun takes flight,
How silly it feels to bask in pure light!

Transparent Secrets

Behind the glass, a mystery brews,
Like hidden giggles or funny clues.
I caught a glimpse of a quirky face,
Making soup in a snail's slow race!

Through frosty panes, I peek and spy,
The world is full of silly highs.
A penguin skating down the street,
In mismatched boots, oh, what a feat!

Windows whisper of secrets bright,
Of robots who try to juggle light.
With a blink and blush, the truth unfurls,
Life is a stage with twists and twirls!

Through clarity, we find the jest,
The joyful sight is often best.
In every glance, the laughter sneaks,
Transparent secrets bring funny weeks!

The Echoing Surface

In a café, drinks all around,
Clinks and clinks make a funny sound.
A splash of coffee, a giggle so bright,
Reflections of laughter, pure delight.

Sipping tea with a twist of lime,
Puns bounce off walls, oh, what a time!
Mirrored missives, witty and wild,
Each sip a joke, like a playful child.

Sugar packets dance on the table,
Kettle's laughter, oh, how it's able!
A little chaos, a lot of cheer,
Tiny mishaps, we hold so dear.

In this glass world where giggles reside,
Fun is reflective, no need to hide.
With every sip, let the jokes fly,
Here in our bubble, laughter won't die.

Prism Pathways

Through rainbow hues a joke takes flight,
Colors collide in a comical sight.
Reflections dance on a sunny day,
Laughter erupts in a playful way.

A slip on the sidewalk, a tumble and roll,
In bright refrains, we find our soul.
Every corner reveals a new tale,
With giggles aplenty, we surely won't fail.

Chasing the light, we trip and we sway,
With each gleam of fun, we'll proudly play.
Lenses of joy in this surreal space,
Prism-lit smiles on each friend's face.

As shadows shift, more laughter's revealed,
Life's hilarity shall never be concealed.
With every twist, our spirits uplift,
In these pathways of prismatic gift.

Shards of Tomorrow

In a room of wonders, the shards appear,
Each piece a memory, bringing us cheer.
Broken laughter, yet so divine,
Reflecting stories with every line.

Cracks in the surface tell funny tales,
Of mishaps and laughter that never pales.
A shard of a joke, a glimmer of fun,
In this mosaic, we've already won.

From splinters of light, we find our way,
Every jolt of laughter, come what may.
Tumbling through moments, a humorous ride,
In this jigsaw of life, we take in our stride.

As we piece together the fragments of bliss,
Each chuckle a reminder not to miss.
In the shards we find tomorrow's light,
With laughter to guide us, shining so bright.

A Spectrum of Thoughts

In a world so colorful, thoughts take form,
Ideas collide, in laughter, they swarm.
From reds to the blues, the giggles explode,
A spectrum of humor in every code.

Painting with jokes, we sketch with delight,
Every twist of wit, a burst of pure light.
Like prisms set free in a jolly parade,
We chase after laughter, never afraid.

From whimsical whispers to raucous cries,
A palette of chuckles fills up the skies.
In moments of mirth, we color outside,
The lines of our worries, where joy can reside.

So let's lift our glasses, to laughter, we toast,
To thoughts that we cherish, and memories most.
In this vast spectrum where smiles come alive,
With joy as our compass, together we'll thrive.

Shards of Light & Vision

Tiny fragments shine bright,
Reflecting laughter's delight.
One lens cracked, but spirits soar,
Who needs perfect? We want more!

Bouncing beams off kitchen walls,
Make silly shadows in the halls.
We see the world in bright arrays,
Through quirky mirrors, weird displays.

A prism flips the dinner plate,
As we debate which way's our fate.
Funky shapes dance in the night,
Our vision blurred, but hearts are light.

Jokes fly fast, like wild confetti,
With each glance, we're feeling zesty.
So, here's to fun through fractured sights,
Laughter leads through all our flights.

Prism of Moments

In life's kaleidoscope we stand,
With jumbled colors, freshly planned.
Each giggle caught in shiny hue,
Turns mundane moments into new.

A splash of giggles, a wink of cheer,
A rainbow flashes, crystal clear.
In silly games our laughter roams,
Reflections of our playful homes.

Through frosted glasses, visions gleam,
As we chase after each bright dream.
With every twist, our smiles bloom,
A prism filled with joy to zoom!

Let's toast to all the fun we find,
In every sparkle, every kind.
Moments caught in fractured light,
Are treasures shining day and night.

The Shine Between Frames

Two pictures framed in jolly cheer,
Capture us living without fear.
In every click, a giggle burst,
Creating memories we rehearse.

The rusty lens with wobbly view,
Shows us antics we thought we knew.
Snapshots taken, smiles abide,
A silly dance, a bumpy ride.

Friends and food all mixed up bright,
Through warped glass, a funny sight.
Each frame a tale, a giggle spree,
In contorted fun, we feel so free.

So here's to life, our joy parade,
In sparkling moments, we've made the grade.
Through every twist in our sweet play,
We see the shine in every way.

Echoes in Transparency

See-through antics fill the room,
With laughter echoing like a tune.
A crystal ball or just a lens?
We glide through giggles, no pretends.

Whispers bounce off every wall,
Invisible jokes that stand tall.
Through distorted sights, we can tell,
That messy fun fits us so well.

A sneaky glance through foggy glass,
Reveals the quirks of our bold sass.
In fragments, echoes of our glee,
Bring smiles that all can clearly see.

So toast to life, with joy profound,
In transparent laughter, we are found.
Through every blur, we find the way,
With echoes ringing night and day.

Mosaic of Moments

In a frame of color bright,
Laughter dances in the light.
Every hue tells a tale,
Of mishaps where we both fail.

Pinks and greens swirl with glee,
A portrait of you and me.
With goofy grins we take a shot,
Captured chaos, quite a lot.

Snaps of joy, oh what a sight,
Turning frowns to pure delight.
A puzzle mixed in every bend,
Laughter echoes, never ends.

Fragments shine, our story told,
In quirky laughs, we find our gold.
Memories framed in colors wild,
Every moment, a silly child.

The Quasar's Gaze

Through quirky lenses, stars collide,
With each blink, a cosmic slide.
Galaxies made of jellybeans,
In this world of wacky scenes.

I squint to see a wobbly star,
Is that a joke, or just bizarre?
Pay attention to the space between,
Where laughter reigns, and we are keen.

Glasses cracked with tales untold,
In laughter we find our hold.
Astronomers in silly threads,
With colorful dreams in our heads.

The universe is but a jest,
In mirrored lenses, we find the best.
So twist that frame and watch with cheer,
For every giggle brings us near.

Captured Illusions

Reflections dance in tiny rings,
Oh, the silly joy that brings.
With every twist, a joke appears,
In the glass, we shed our fears.

A wink reveals a funny sight,
Where shadows play in pure delight.
Caught in laughter, smiles ignite,
Like fireflies in the night.

Mirrors laughing back at me,
With goofy faces, wild and free.
Each glance a snapshot of a tie,
And in that moment, I can fly.

Through mirrored glances, fun unfolds,
Stories spun in shimmering golds.
Captured moments a sweet illusion,
With laughter as our grand conclusion.

Enigmatic Reflections

Silly faces in the glass,
I chuckle hard, as you just pass.
With every grin, a secret shared,
In this fun house, nothing's spare.

Reflections twist and turn awry,
Our laughter echoes to the sky.
Wrapped in mirth, the truth's obscure,
In these moments, we find a cure.

A wink, a nod, the glass replies,
With every joke, the world defies.
Where echoes sing in playful tease,
In mirrored realms, we do as we please.

So let's embrace this funny game,
With every glance, a spark of fame.
In our reflections, stories bloom,
In cracks and quirks, we find our room.

Spectrum of Emotions

Through lenses thick, I see the world,
A squirrel dances, my laughter swirled.
Colors collide in a playful spree,
My glasses giggle, they smile at me.

Fuzzy faces and quirky sights,
A jester's hat, oh, what a fright!
Each tilt and turn brings joy anew,
These frames hold secrets, not just a view.

Lenses play tricks on my blinkered mind,
An owl in a tux, how could it be blind?
They shimmer and shine with a cheeky flare,
Making the mundane a captivating dare.

As I wander through this whimsical haze,
My vision's warped in delightful ways.
A hat on a cat? What a sight to behold!
With every glance, a new story told.

The Gaze that Transcends

These stylish specs have a mind of their own,
Leading me places I've never been shown.
A duck in a dress? Oh, what a surprise!
Each gaze a riddle, no need for the wise.

They frame the world with a humorous spin,
Turning dull moments to chuckles within.
When I wink at shadows and squint at the sun,
Laughter erupts, oh, what mischief I've won!

I'm wearing a rainbow, just watch me glide,
With a flick of the wrist, I'm a whimsical slide.
Every giggle captured through panes of delight,
Even the cats wear monocles tonight!

So here's to the lenses that shape our laughs,
In this spectacle world, let's take goofy paths.
For every glimpse deepens the humor we share,
Through quirks of reflection, we'll dance in mid-air.

Tapestry of Transparency

In a world of clarity, find the bizarre,
An elephant prances, oh what a star!
Frames full of fun, each glance a new twist,
Whimsy waltzes where logic gets kissed.

With lenses that sparkle like bubbles in air,
A frog in a tux, struts with flair!
Cups of giggles poured over our heads,
Laughter like confetti, joylessly spreads.

Look over there, a chicken in jeans,
Squawking its fashion, a sight fit for queens!
Every perspective invites more delight,
Each peek through the glass makes the mundane take flight.

Through colors and shapes, every glance reveals,
The extraordinary truth that laughter conceals.
What fun can erupt from a simple clear gaze,
In the tapestry woven of humorous plays!

Cascading Reflections

Reflections cascade like a waterfall bright,
A clown on a tricycle, what a weird sight!
Mirrors hold tales of the wacky and wild,
Every glance back, I'm the giggling child.

Through frames that boggle, reality bends,
A toaster with feet, oh, where does it end?
Each laugh expands, like bubbles in flight,
Twinkling at moments that sparkle with light.

Wearing laughter like it's a crown on my head,
A porcupine brimming with laughter and dread.
These spectacles serve up a feast for my eyes,
With joy overflowing, no room for goodbyes.

So onward I venture with glasses of glee,
Embracing the whimsy, oh let it be free!
In this grand carnival that life has designed,
Every shimmering glance leaves sweet humor behind.

Focusing on Fleeting Truths

In a bar, laughs ricochet,
Witty remarks dance and sway.
Who needs vision? We just guess,
A toast to truth's wild, blurry mess.

One friend's nose becomes a star,
A spectacle—from here, not far.
Another thinks he's far too wise,
Winking with both of his eyes.

We squint and sip our fizzy cheer,
Crafty tales echo, loud and clear.
Those elusive answers fly,
When jests and jibes make spirits high.

The evening sways, a nonsensical ruse,
With every sip, our sight we lose.
Yet woven laughter can't be beat,
In this merry muddle, we find our seat.

Brightening Shadows

In shadows long, a mystery brews,
With glasses thick, we search for clues.
"Is that a cat, or just a hat?"
We ponder deep—imagine that!

A friend insists his drink is bold,
Yet in his hand, a mug of gold.
He swears it's tea, we call it wine,
Each sip is laced with sparkle and shine.

Mismatched socks command the floor,
While witty banter opens the door.
As glares illuminate our silly ways,
We stumble on truths, just for a phase.

The room ignites with playful charm,
In blurry light, we twist and harm.
When laughter echoes, shadows play,
We toast to visions gone astray.

Clarity's Embrace

What clarity lies in blurry sight?
We squint our eyes, who needs the light?
A menu reads like ancient lore,
As we guess dishes and beg for more.

My drink appears with a twist and shout,
Is it gin, or what, I've got no doubt.
Laughter bubbles in fizzy glaze,
Lost in our little, silly maze.

Whose voice is louder? A conundrum grows,
As stories fumble, the punchline lopes.
In this laughter-filled, jumbled sea,
Each mistake's a gem; must we wear them free?

So here we toast amidst the throng,
For clarity's sweet, just a bit wrong.
In playful haze, we'll find our grace,
With a giggle and love's warm embrace.

Spectral Vignettes

Through glasses thick, the world's a jest,
With every glance, we're put to the test.
Each reflection a peculiar sight,
A dancing ghost in the night.

A wild sandwich claims the plate,
Is it lunchtime or is it fate?
We munch and crunch, the flavors blend,
As chewy tales and winked grins send.

A toast to mischief, a laugh for fun,
The night extends, filled with puns.
In spectral hues, we break our binds,
Bound by whims, our laughter reminds.

So let us cheer for the curious quest,
In a blurry truth, we find our best.
With every chuckle, let spirits fly,
In joyful tales, we'll never die!

www.ingramcontent.com/pod-product-compliance
Lightning Source LLC
Chambersburg PA
CBHW071126130526
44590CB00056B/2720